WISE SAYINGS

from

PROVERBS

WISE SAYINGS

from

PROVERBS

LION

Compiled by Olivia Warburton
This edition copyright © 2011 Lion Hudson
The author asserts the moral right
to be identified as the author of this work

A Lion Book
an imprint of
Lion Hudson plc
Wilkinson House, Jordan Hill Road,
Oxford OX2 8DR, England
www.lionhudson.com
ISBN 978 0 7459 5553 7

Distributed by:
UK: Marston Book Services, PO Box 269,
Abingdon, Oxon, OX14 4YN
USA: Trafalgar Square Publishing, 814 N.
Franklin Street, Chicago, IL 60610
USA Christian Market: Kregel Publications,
PO Box 2607, Grand Rapids, MI 49501

First edition 2011
10 9 8 7 6 5 4 3 2 1 0

Acknowledgments
pp. 14t, 20b, 34t, 38, 42b, 45, 48b, 52b, 55b,
58m: Scripture quotations are from *The Holy
Bible, English Standard Version*, published by
HarperCollins Publishers, copyright © 2001
Crossway Bibles, a division of Good News
Publishers. Used by permission. All rights
reserved. pp. 23t, 24t, 30b, 32b, 35t, 36t,
42t, 47t, 49, 56t: Scripture quotations are
from the *Good News Bible* published by the
Bible Societies and HarperCollins Publishers,
© American Bible Society 1994, used with
permission. pp. 12, 14b, 15b, 21, 22, 26, 31t,
32t, 34b, 35b, 36m, 43b, 52t, 55t, 56b, 58b:
Scripture quotations taken from the *Holy Bible,
New International Version*, copyright © 1973,
1978, 1984 International Bible Society. Used
by permission of Zondervan and Hodder
& Stoughton Limited. All rights reserved.
The 'NIV' and 'New International Version'
trademarks are registered in the United States
Patent and Trademark Office by International
Bible Society. Use of either trademark
requires the permission of International Bible
Society. UK trademark number 1448790.

pp. 13, 15t, 16, 25, 30t, 33, 37, 44, 46t, 48t:
The New King James Version copyright © 1982,
1979 by Thomas Nelson, Inc. J.B. Phillips
Reprinted with the permission of Simon &
Schuster from *The New Testament in Modern
English, Revised Edition*, translated by
J. B. Phillips. Copyright © 1958, 1960, 1972
by J. B. Phillips. Reprinted from *The New
Testament in Modern English, Revised Edition*,
translated by J.B. Phillips. Published by
HarperCollins Publishers Ltd. pp. 6, 10,
11, 20t, 24b, 31b, 47b, 53t, 54t, 57t, 58t:
Scripture quotations are taken from the *Holy
Bible, New Living Translation*, copyright ©
1996. Used by permission of Tyndale House
Publishers, Inc., Wheaton, Illinois 60189.
All rights reserved. pp. 23b, 27, 36b, 39, 43t,
46b, 53b, 54b, 57b, 59: Scripture quotations
are from the *New Revised Standard Version*
published by HarperCollins Publishers,
copyright © 1989 by the Division of Christian
Education of the National Council of the
Churches of Christ in the USA, and are used
by permission.
All rights reserved.

A catalogue record for this book is available
from the British Library
Typeset in 10.5/12 Perpetua and 10/24
Zapfino
Printed and bound in China

ONTENTS

INTRODUCTION

Throughout the ages the Proverbs have been celebrated for their spiritual insight and ability to speak to the heart of the human condition.

This collection brings together passages from this unique work of wisdom literature. By exploring a range of issues – whether justice or simple living, decision-making or how to know God – and contrasting right with wrong, these ancient writings point us towards the best way to shape our lives.

How much better to get wisdom than gold, and good judgment than silver!

PROVERBS 16:16

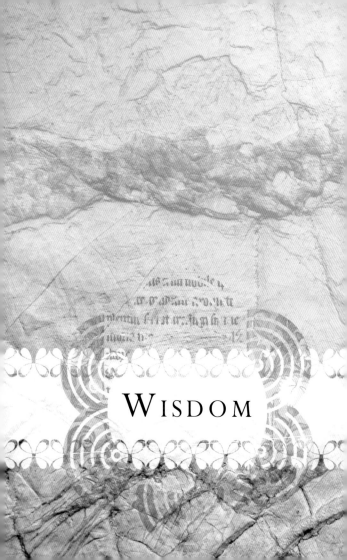

WISDOM

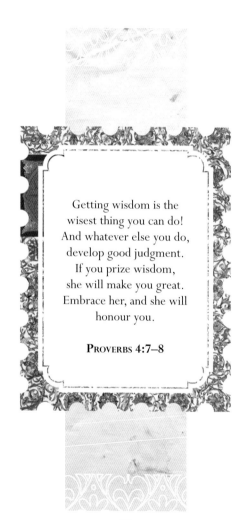

Getting wisdom is the
wisest thing you can do!
And whatever else you do,
develop good judgment.
If you prize wisdom,
she will make you great.
Embrace her, and she will
honour you.

PROVERBS 4:7–8

My child, listen to what I say,
and treasure my commands.
Tune your ears to wisdom,
and concentrate on understanding.
Cry out for insight,
and ask for understanding.
Search for them as you would for silver;
seek them like hidden treasures.
Then you will understand what
it means to fear the Lord,
and you will gain knowledge of God.
For the Lord grants wisdom!
From his mouth come knowledge and understanding.
He grants a treasure of common sense to the honest.
He is a shield to those who walk with integrity.
He guards the paths of the just
and protects those who are faithful to him.

PROVERBS 2:1–8

Wisdom has built her house;
she has set up its seven pillars.
She has prepared her meat
and mixed her wine;
she has also set her table.
She has sent out her servants, and she calls
from the highest point of the city,
"Let all who are simple come to my house!"
To those who have no sense she says,
"Come, eat my food
and drink the wine I have mixed.
Leave your simple ways and you will live;
walk in the way of insight."

PROVERBS 9:1–6

Through wisdom
a house is built,
And by understanding
it is established;
By knowledge
the rooms are filled
With all precious
and pleasant riches.

PROVERBS 24:3–4

Listen to advice and accept instruction,
that you may gain wisdom in the future.

PROVERBS 19:20

Start children off
on the way they should go,
and even when they are old
they will not turn from it.

PROVERBS 22:6

He who earnestly seeks
good finds favour,
But trouble will come
to him who seeks evil.

PROVERBS 11:27

The one who has knowledge uses words with restraint,
and whoever has understanding is even-tempered.
Even fools are thought wise if they keep silent,
and discerning if they hold their tongues.

PROVERBS 17:27–28

Happy is the man who finds wisdom,
And the man who gains understanding;
For her proceeds are better than the profits of silver,
And her gain than fine gold.
She is more precious than rubies,
And all the things you may desire
cannot compare with her.
Length of days is in her right hand,
In her left hand riches and honour.
Her ways are ways of pleasantness,
And all her paths are peace.
She is a tree of life to those who take hold of her,
And happy are all who retain her.

PROVERBS 3:13–18

fine gold

INTEGRITY

The way of the righteous is like the first gleam of dawn,
which shines ever brighter until the full light of day.

PROVERBS 4:18

*Whoever walks in integrity
walks securely,
but he who makes his ways
crooked will be found out.*

PROVERBS 10:9

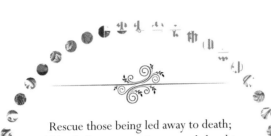

Rescue those being led away to death;
hold back those staggering toward slaughter.
If you say, "But we knew nothing about this,"
does not he who weighs the heart perceive it?
Does not he who guards your life know it?
Will he not repay each person according
to what he has done?

PROVERBS 24:11–12

There are six things the Lord hates,
seven that are detestable to him:
haughty eyes,
a lying tongue,
hands that shed innocent blood,
a heart that devises wicked schemes,
feet that are quick to rush into evil,
a false witness who pours out lies
and a person who stirs up conflict in
the community.

PROVERBS 6:16–19

Do what is right and fair;
that pleases the Lord more
than bringing him sacrifices.

PROVERBS 21:3

Speak out for those who cannot speak,
for the rights of all the destitute.
Speak out, judge righteously,
defend the rights of the poor and needy.

PROVERBS 31:8–9

If you oppress poor people,
you insult the God who made them;
but kindness shown to the poor
is an act of worship.

PROVERBS 14:31

Those who shut their ears
to the cries of the poor will be ignored
in their own time of need.

PROVERBS 21:13

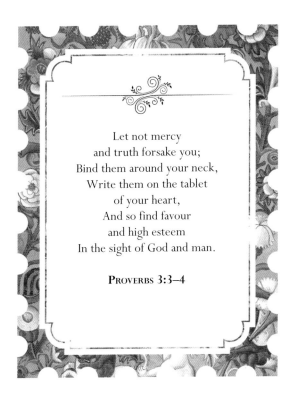

Let not mercy
and truth forsake you;
Bind them around your neck,
Write them on the tablet
of your heart,
And so find favour
and high esteem
In the sight of God and man.

PROVERBS 3:3–4

All a person's ways seem pure to them,
but motives are weighed by the Lord.

PROVERBS 16:2

No one can be established
through wickedness,
but the righteous cannot
be uprooted.

PROVERBS 12:3

springs of

Keep your heart with all vigilance,
for from it flow the springs of life.

PROVERBS 4:23

life

CHOICES

If your enemy is hungry, give him bread to eat;
And if he is thirsty, give him water to drink;
For so you will heap coals of fire on his head,
And the Lord will reward you.

PROVERBS 25:21–22

*Don't be glad when your
enemies meet disaster,
and don't rejoice when
they stumble.*

PROVERBS 24:17

Do not withhold good from those to whom it is due,
when it is in your power to act.
Do not say to your neighbour,
"Come back tomorrow and I'll give it to you" –
when you already have it with you.

PROVERBS 3:27–28

A gracious woman gains respect,
but ruthless men gain only wealth.

PROVERBS 11:16

Starting a quarrel is like breaching a dam;
so drop the matter before a dispute breaks out.

PROVERBS 17:14

Don't take it on yourself

to repay a wrong.

Trust the Lord and he will

make it right.

PROVERBS 20:22

Whoever digs a pit
will fall into it,
And he who rolls a stone will
have it roll back on him.

PROVERBS 26:27

Hatred stirs up strife,
But love covers all sins.

PROVERBS 10:12

A man without self-control is like
a city broken into and left without walls.

PROVERBS 25:28

Do not make friends with a hot-tempered person,
do not associate with one easily angered,
or you may learn their ways
and get yourself ensnared.

PROVERBS 22:24–25

A gossip can never keep a secret.
Stay away from people who talk too much.

PROVERBS 20:19

*Like a muddied spring
or a polluted well
are the righteous who give
way to the wicked.*

PROVERBS 25:26

Let other people praise you
— even strangers;
never do it yourself.

PROVERBS 27:2

*The crucible for silver
and the furnace for gold,
but people are tested by their praise.*

PROVERBS 27:21

One who gives
an honest answer
gives a kiss on the lips.

PROVERBS 24:26

Pleasant words are
like a honeycomb,
Sweetness to the soul
and health to the bones.

PROVERBS 16:24

If one curses his father
or his mother,
his lamp will be put out
in utter darkness.

PROVERBS 20:20

Fools show their anger at once,
but the prudent ignore an insult....
Rash words are like sword thrusts,
but the tongue of the wise
brings healing.

Proverbs 12:16, 18

MONEY

The rich and the poor have this in common:
the Lord made them both.

PROVERBS 22:2

Two things I ask of you;
deny them not to me before I die:
Remove far from me falsehood and lying;
give me neither poverty nor riches;
feed me with the food that is needful for me,
lest I be full and deny you
and say, "Who is the Lord?"
or lest I be poor and steal
and profane the name of my God.

PROVERBS 30:7–9

Some give freely, yet grow all the richer;
    others withhold what is due,
        and only suffer want.
A generous person will be enriched,
    and one who gives water will get water.

Proverbs 11:24–25

Do not eat the food of a begrudging host,
    do not crave his delicacies;
    for he is the kind of person
who is always thinking about the cost.
    "Eat and drink," he says to you,
        but his heart is not with you.

Proverbs 23:6–7

Go to the ant, you sluggard!
Consider her ways
and be wise,
Which, having no captain,
Overseer or ruler,
Provides her supplies
in the summer,
And gathers her food
in the harvest.

PROVERBS 6:6–8

I passed by the field of a sluggard,
by the vineyard of a man lacking sense,
and behold, it was all overgrown with thorns;
the ground was covered with nettles,
and its stone wall was broken down.
Then I saw and considered it;
I looked and received instruction.
A little sleep, a little slumber,
a little folding of the hands to rest,
and poverty will come upon you like a robber,
and want like an armed man.

PROVERBS 24:30–34

Better is a dry morsel
with quietness,
Than a house full of feasting
with strife.

PROVERBS 17:1

Do not wear yourself out to get rich;
be wise enough to desist.
When your eyes light upon it, it is gone;
for suddenly it takes wings to itself,
flying like an eagle towards heaven.

PROVERBS 23:4–5

Never boast about tomorrow.
You don't know what will happen
between now and then.

PROVERBS 27:1

Honour the Lord with your wealth
and with the best part of everything you produce.
Then he will fill your barns with grain,
and your vats will overflow with good wine.

PROVERBS 3:9–10

A good name is to be chosen
rather than great riches,
Loving favour rather than
silver and gold.

PROVERBS 22:1

Whoever trusts in his riches will fall,
but the righteous will flourish like
a green leaf.

PROVERBS 11:28

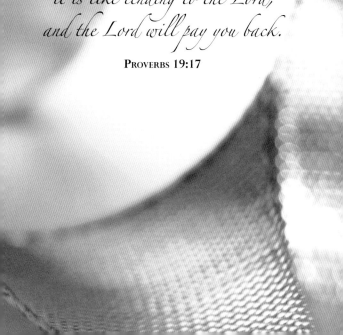

When you give to the poor,
it is like lending to the Lord,
and the Lord will pay you back.

PROVERBS 19:17

SECURITY